The Ultimate Guide to

Classroom Racism

Management

"THESE KIDS ARE DRIVING ME NUTS! This year has been filled with so many classroom disruptions - the students have been involved in excessive talking, talking back, insubordination, clowning and making jokes, using the word 'nigger,' walking into my class without permission, and a number of other violations. I have used numerous resources and the classroom disruptions continue. Is my classroom management techniques really that bad?" asked Mrs. Thompson. If this is you, then you have arrived at the right place. If you want to avoid this from becoming you, then you have also arrived at the right place.

The Ultimate Guide to Classroom Racism Management helps teachers to refine their classroom management skills to ensure that racism is not a factor that contributes to classroom disruptions. Classroom disruptions interrupt either the teacher's ability to teach or student's right to learn, and when students are not learning, the perception is that it is the teacher's fault. Without this book, many teachers will continue to struggle with their classroom management techniques which ultimately impacts the progress for the entire school.

A recent investigation revealed that classroom disruptions contributed to an increase in disciplinary infractions and a decrease in student achievement. Like many schools, the staff demographics do not replicate the student dynamics. The administrator demographics for this study were 67% White and 33% Black. The instructional staff demographics were 97% White, 3% Black, and 2% Hispanic, and student demographics were 60% Hispanic, 33% Black, 4% White, and 3% Asian Pacific Islander. In addition, 99% of the students qualified for reduced or free lunch. In this study, most teachers were White and most students were Hispanic and Black.

Minority student suspensions were overrepresented at this school. The student suspension rate was 29%, 24.2%, and 25.4% for three academic years, while the state averages were 13.8%, 12.9%, and 15.3% respectively. Processed disciplinary infractions revealed that Black students were overrepresented. Black students accounted for 45% of the processed disciplinary infractions while only accounting for 33% of the student population. Hispanic, White, and Asian students accounted for 53%, 1%, and 1% of the processed disciplinary infractions, respectively. Teacher-student interactions accounted for 70% of the discipline referrals, and within this 70%, discipline referral quantities included 40% disrupting class, 28% disrespect toward a staff member, 23% open defiance, and 9% other infractions. The majority of the disciplinary infractions were related to interactions between teachers and students.

Black students will continue to carry their own culture into the classroom, and they will continue to misunderstand their middle-class teacher as profoundly as she or he will misunderstand them. The classroom conflict between teachers and students results from the different cultural contexts that students and teachers bring to the classroom, yet quality teacher-student interactions are one of the most important variables that influence student achievement in the classroom.

Schools that have high quantities of classroom disruptions also have low student achievement, low attendance rates which also impact graduation rates, and increased discipline. Schools can improve by eliminating classroom clashes between teachers and students which result from classroom disruptions. This process must begin by providing teachers with Classroom Racism Management strategies.

The book, "The Ultimate Guide to Classroom Racism Management," is comprised of several chapters, and each chapter will help educators to better understand the dynamics associated with successfully managing classroom racism. This guide is consistent of the classroom management aspects that many educators fail to learn before they enter the classroom.

"The Ultimate Classroom Racism Management Guide" helps teachers to understand how racism plays a major role in the classroom. The following chapters cover the primary elements that contribute to better managing classroom racism along with solutions to different classroom racial challenges.

The intended audience for this book is teachers. I wish the teachers who read this book joy, happiness, and continued success as they implement the techniques outlined in this book.

Other Works by Dr. Derrick L. Campbell

Books
- *Promoting Positive Racial Teacher Student Classroom Relationships*
- *Promoting Positive Racial Teacher Student Classroom Relationships: Workbook*
- *Promoting Positive Racial Teacher Student Classroom Relationships: Methodology*
- *Leading Your Marriage into the Promised Land*
- *Leading Your Marriage into the Promised Land: Workbook for Husbands*
- *Leading Your Marriage into the Promised Land: Workbook for Wives*
- *Advanced Marriage Training for Singles*
- *Husband Leadership Principles*
- *Advanced Marriage Training for Couples: Workbook*
- *treasures of Hidden Racism in Education*

Education Articles
- *Cultural Influences: Differences in Teacher Perspectives*
- *Developing Student Recognition Programs for Historically Underserved Students*
- *Ethical Leadership Develops Moral Communities*
- *Firing the Principal Does Not Guarantee Improvement*
- *Leadership Qualities that Promote Positive Racial Teacher-Student Relationships*
- *Poverty: The Assumed Link to Low Minority Student Achievement*
- *Reducing Cultural Bullying in Schools*
- *Reducing Cultural Challenges Saves Money*
- *Reducing Inappropriate Special Education Referrals for Historically Underserved Students*
- *Save Money by Reducing Student Suspensions*
- *Smile: They Like It*
- *Steering the Organizational Change Process*
- *Student Input is the Key to Effective Classroom Management*
- *Student Perspectives of Classroom Disruptions*
- *Students Need Professional Development Too*
- *Students Who Promote Positive Racial Teacher-Student Classroom Relationships: Part 1*
- *Students Who Promote Positive Racial Teacher-Student Classroom Relationships: Part 2*
- *Teacher Perspectives of Classroom Disruptions*
- *Teacher Qualities that Promote Positive Racial Classroom Relationships*
- *Transforming Afro-American Content into the School Curriculum*
- *Unions Can Benefit Organizational Change*
- *Classroom Management Strategies*

The Ultimate Guide to Classroom Racism Management

Dr. Derrick L. Campbell, Ed.D.

DLC Consultant Group

All rights reserved. No part of this book may be reproduced in any form or by any electronic or mechanical means, including information storage and retrieval systems, without permission in writing from the publisher, except by a reviewer who may quote brief passages in a review.

Published by Derrick L. Campbell

First edition: June, 2017

ISBN: 978-0-9975052-2-1

Printed in the United States of America

TABLE OF CONTENTS

Page

ABOUT THE AUTHOR x

Chapter

I. CLASSROOM DISRUPTIONS 1

II. DISRUPTIVE MENTALITY 23

III. CIVIL RIGHTS IMPASSE 39

IV. THE RACCELERATE FORMULA 53

V. CLASSROOM COMMUNICATION 65

VI. REFERENCES 115

ABOUT THE AUTHOR

Dr. Campbell holds a Bachelor of Science degree in Electronics Engineering Technology from Capital Institute of Technology, a second Bachelor of Science degree in Math Education from the University of the District of Columbia, a Masters in Education Administration from Lincoln University, and a doctoral degree in Educational Leadership from Rowan University.

He is also the founder and CEO of DLC Consultant Group. After authoring his first book, Promoting Positive Racial Teacher-Student Classroom Relationships, in January 2008, Dr. Campbell developed a Cultural Relationship Training Program that improves teacher-student classroom relationships as well as several companion programs. He also developed the B.O.S.S. Leadership Training Program that improves manager-employee workplace relationships and relationships between Law Enforcement and their local community.

Dr. Campbell authored his second book, Leading Your Marriage into the Promised Land, in February 2009. Leading Your Marriage into the Promised Land educates the husband on a leadership process that ensures the husband and wife work together as a team. The husband and wife work together to develop and implement agreed upon goals that embrace the different values that they learn as children. Following the writing of this book, he wrote two companion workbooks, one for husbands and the other for wives.

Dr. Campbell authored his fifth book - Advanced Marriage Training for Singles - in September, 2014. Advanced Marriage Training for Singles better equips singles to make informed decisions about who they marry before they decide to become engaged.

In 2016, he authored Advanced Marriage Training for Couples: Workbook and Husband Leadership Principles.

Dr. Campbell is founder and president of The Promised Land Ministry. The Promised Land Ministry provides training for churches, non-profit organizations, men, and couples. Churches and non-profit organizations receive training in the areas of strategic planning, team building, and leadership.

In August 2007, Dr. Campbell founded Leadership Advancement Journal which publishes articles on recent educational, organizational, and business developments that impact our culture. His articles, Reducing Cultural Bullying in Schools and Reducing Inappropriate Special Education Referrals for Historically Underserved Students, have been featured in a local New Jersey newspaper.

In November 2008, Dr. Campbell began the new Radio talk show - Culturally Speaking with Doctor Derrick. On this talk show we discuss the solutions to the cultural challenges that exist in our schools, workplaces, and community. Dr. Campbell has had a host of local and national speakers who contributed to the content of the show.

Dr. Campbell has lectured at various locations throughout the nation, including the National Association for the Advancement of Colored People (NAACP), Iron Sharpens Iron Men's Conference, and local churches. He has ministered to the youth at his home church on the topic of Christian student rights in the public schools and has ministered at another local New Jersey church on Overcoming the Poverty Cycle. He has been a board member of his church's men's ministry, Athletes United in Christ, and has participated in various church activities. He has facilitated Leading Your Marriage into the Promised seminars at churches and the Iron Sharpens Iron Conference Men's Conference.

CLASSROOM DISRUPTIONS

Successful classroom racism management requires that teachers become the experts at eliminating classroom disruptions associated with racism. Before a teacher can become an expert in classroom racism management, they must understand how racism can play a major role in classroom disruptions. Teachers can reach all of their students when they understand the ways in which culture influences the educational process in schools and within their classroom.

The most common classroom infractions are talking, inappropriate use of materials, and inappropriate movement. Many teachers respond to these infractions by ordering, reprimanding, involving the students in work, or naming the student; these tactics are known to lead to classroom disruptions when the lack of cultural knowledge plays a major role.

In Youngstown, Ohio for example, a teacher has been charged with assault that resulted from a classroom disruption. The disruption began when a Life Skills student refused the teachers request for the student's laptop. The teacher confiscated the laptop, and the student pursued the teacher, resulting in a fist fight between the teacher and student. The teacher was then arrested and charged with assault.

Once the teacher confiscated the student's laptop, the teacher validated the students cultural perception of schools as Black students learn at an early age to be wary of people and systems in their environment. Teacher-student conflicts result from a difference in desires, and even though this difference may be reduced, it will remain in schools without better teacher preparation. Teachers must have better preparation to ensure that they are not penalized or victimized by classroom disruptions.

In a recent study, both teachers and students elaborated on the causes and responses to classroom disruptions. One teacher described classroom disruptions as an act related to student behavior. This teacher stated:

> "If someone who gets up and walks around the room, you have to tell them to sit down. Somebody who is constantly talking about something other than what they are supposed to be doing and bothering another student, or somebody who is just sitting there and looking around the room, and they are not really doing anything. They are disrupting themselves."

If this student was Black, then this teacher would benefit from the research regarding Black student classroom behavior. Before Black students begin a task, they may look over the assignment in its entirety, rearrange their posture and writing space, ask the teacher to repeat the directions, check the perception of other neighboring students, and check pencils and paper. For Black students, these are necessary classroom behaviors while teachers may perceive that the students are inattentive, disruptive, not prepared, or attempting to avoid completing the task.

Teachers also indicated that most classroom disruptions result from talking. Black students have classroom talking behaviors that result from interest in the instructional process. They are inclined to talk back when motivated by what a teacher says, and may become so impressed with the speaker, such as a teacher, that the students want to hear the teacher again due to an interest, not in what was said, but how it was said. Many Black students want to create the appropriate mood and setting before beginning to work on a task by asking the teacher to repeat the directions. Black students want gratification for classroom efforts, and will argue for recognition of unsuccessful efforts toward completing a task. Many teachers do not expect Black students to interrupt the class by talking to their neighbors and speaking without raising their hands because educators assume that quiet students are successful and receive rewards for making teaching an easier task.

In this same study, teachers responded to students talking in the classroom without permission by ordering, reprimanding, involving students in work, or naming the student. Some teachers may exhibit unprofessional behavior when students talk in the classroom without permission. When a teacher yells, uses harsh words, shames, degrades, or embarrasses a student, such behavior influences all students.

Some teachers were also unfamiliar with minority student verbal behavior. One teacher stated:

> "Two students decided to talk about a situation in the classroom, and it escalated to two, three, and four other students. Then, the two students were talking, and one student said to the other one something and the other one became angry, and threw a piece of paper at the other student."

Puerto Ricans have verbal behavior that is consistent with this teacher's description. Puerto Rican students use indirectas, a form of speech that is an indirect way of making something known. According to Morris (1981):

> "Indirectas are literally, indirect statements critical of others—insinuations, innuendo. They are

disguised or purposely vague to any but the initiated, but clear in meaning to the ones who know the circumstance or the people involved. In form they do not give away either the person speaking or the person spoken of; they seem not to be barbed and directed to particulars, but they are meaningful in context. Anyone who is "in the know" does know how they are to be applied (p. 102)."

Interviewed teachers expressed their frustration with students who interrupt the class by talking without permission. One teacher stated:

> "We were having an active class, [and] everybody was participating. One of the students was just talking. He was continuously talking, and I said 'could you please be quiet?' He kept talking. He was talking with another student. The other student was quiet and paying attention. He was talking, and

turning around. and just not still. I asked [him] a question, and he just ignored me. I know he heard me, but he just ignored me. I asked [him] the question again, and he ignored me again. I told him, 'you have to pay attention when we are doing something so get back to work.' He kept talking."

Another teacher stated:

"He was just talking, and turning around, and not paying attention. He did not want to participate either. Then, I asked him to participate and he refused. He just ignored me, as if he did not hear me."

Students frequently test the limitations in an inconsistent classroom by ignoring a teacher's first, second, and even third request for compliance. When the teacher decides to deliver a consequence, the student claims the teacher is unfair because the same misbehavior does not always receive the same consequence.

Some students are resistant and refuse to comply with a teacher's request, and teachers who use coercion, an attempt to manage students by applying sanctions such as detention, suspension, and corporal punishment, are ineffective. Resistant students view this as the boss using coercion and become the teacher's adversary.

It appears that resistant students across the world have a negative response to corporal punishment. In New Delhi, India, a teacher was scolding a student for alleged poor classroom behavior. The student became resistant, and the teacher responded by slapping the student to which the student responded by slapping the teacher back. The incident escalated and the teacher and student got into a fight, and the student reacted to the teacher's disciplinary assertiveness which is consistent with the behavior of some Black students.

Black students react to arbitrary and autocratic White teacher disciplinary assertiveness by believing that a White man is still trying to tell them what to do. Likewise, most teachers respond to students who attempt to act tough with them by threatening or talking back to the student. Removing hostile Black students from the classroom only delays the inevitable confrontation between the teacher and the student. Whites attempt to minimize confrontations and struggles with Blacks in the persuasive process that they interpret as divisive while Blacks believe these struggles unify because they care enough to struggle for something. Abrahams and Gay (1975) reported:

> "If a [Black student] expects to rise to the position of a leader, he must know how to keep his cool. If he cannot respond to a [teacher's challenge] without

becoming frustrated and unnerved, he is not likely to have the respect of others or remain a leader for long (p. 205)."

"When Blacks are working hard to keep it cool, it signals that the chasm between is getting wider, not smaller" (McCarty, 1981, p. 20). According to Gay (2000), Black students "gain the floor" or get participatory entry into conversations through personal assertiveness, the strength of the impulse to be involved, and persuasive power of the point they wish to make rather than waiting for "authority" to grant permission (p. 91). In the classroom, Black students' power play by talking loudly or back talking to make the teacher lose his or her cool and get the last word in.

In the same study, teachers reported that disruptive behavior was the second most common classroom disruption source. Two teachers reported fighting and bullying disrupted their class, and one teacher stated that, "In the past, I have had a few girls fighting in my classroom, and I had to write both students up." Another teacher stated, "There was one time, I sent a student down to the Assistant Principal's Office because he was disrupting the classroom and hitting other students."

Teachers and students reported that classroom disruptions result from insubordination. A teacher stated:

> "A student was not willing to participate in the learning activity that was taking place by being obstinate, putting her head down, talking back, and not being compliant in joining the group in a discussion."

Hispanic students may have difficulty participating in instructional activities that require them to provide verbal feedback.

According to the same study, a third source of classroom disruptions was insubordination. A teacher recalled a student insubordination act and stated:

> "She refused to read. I offered her a book; it is one of the DEAR books. She just did not want to read, and [I said] that is the requirement for the whole school. So, I ended up writing her up."

A student reported, "We got into an argument because I did not want to do my work." These students could have felt embarrassed by the teacher's request for compliance.

Many students reported that they felt like victims when involved in classroom disruptions. They claimed that teachers made students feel like victims by refusing to repeat instructional expectations, yelling at them in the presence of other students, and responding to them sarcastically. Sarcasm can damage teacher-student relationships as children believe sarcastic messages are negative. Some teachers believe sarcasm may psychologically damage children.

Sarcasm and ridicule "may serve a corrective function, the long-term consequence of diminished esteem in the eyes of students may make the immediate gains in terms of behavioral correction not worth the costs" (Bryant & Zillman, 1988, p. 72). In addition, interviews with high school students removed for behavioral challenges indicated that antagonistic and humiliating teacher behaviors include responding sarcastically. Teacher awareness regarding Black and Hispanic student classroom behavior would help teachers to understand students.

In response to teacher sarcasm, another student stated:

> "We were sitting and joking around in the classroom, and the teacher says something to me real funny, like he was joking around or whatever. Then, I came back and I said a joke back to him, and he did not take it as like when he told me the joke. So, he got mad. He told me to go down to the office, and he wrote me up."

Teachers who use irrelevant jokes and humor reduce instructional time. Blacks and Mexican Americans verbally communicate by using jokes and humor, therefore, teachers must use humor naturally, or else it can backfire. Mexican Americans use jokes and humor to avoid disagreements.

In this study, students reported various responses to classroom disruptions. One student stated, "That just made me angry. I just flipped. The whole class looked at me as if they never see me react like that." Another student stated, "The teacher said be quiet. The students took it as another point of view. She just got mad over nothing."

In another incident, a student recalled that classmates cheered his disruptive behavior. Similarly, a teacher reported that students enjoy when teachers respond to classroom disruptions by becoming upset. The teacher stated, "I found that last year . . . I got upset with them. I [would say], 'How dare you treat me like this! Don't you know you are being rude?' And when I got angry, it just elevated their bad attitude."

Some students employ strategies that will upset the classroom environment. For instance, Black students use several verbal techniques to discover a teacher's strengths and weaknesses in order to evaluate teachers' racial attitudes and hopefully find their breaking points to help empower themselves in situations between them and the teacher. Abrahams and Gay (1972) reported:

> "If a [Black student] expects to rise to the position of a leader, he must know how to keep his cool. If he cannot respond to a [teachers challenge] without becoming frustrated and unnerved, he is not likely to have the respect of others or remain a leader for long (p. 205)."

In the classroom, Black students power play by talking loudly or back talking to make teachers lose their cool and get the last word in.

Not only did students admit to employing strategies that upset the classroom environment, but they also gave recommendations for students to eliminate involvement in classroom disruptions. One student stated, "Mind your business; that should be the first rule about everything. Mind your business; it does not have anything to do with you." Another student stated:

> "Just be patient and wait till [the teacher] comes to you. Do not sit there asking her [questions] because it is going to make her even more mad. [It is] going to make you even more mad because she is going to give you an answer that you do not want to hear. She is going to keep on telling you to wait, [but] you do not want hear [that]. You do not want to hear nothing. It is nothing but patience."

This student may have believed that the teacher enjoyed helping all students and that he would have to wait for his turn. High school students believe effective teachers enjoy helping students.

While some students developed classroom strategies to control their disruptive behaviors, some teachers responded to students who talked excessively in the classroom by using verbal communication. One teacher stated, "I tell them, 'I am not arguing with you.' I will look at them and say, 'Are you arguing with me? Do not argue with me.' I say it in that tone – 'Do not argue with me.'" Another teacher agreed and stated, "I don't get into the back and forth."

Arguments have different meanings for different cultures. For Whites, the purpose of an argument is to ventilate anger and hostility, however, "Blacks distinguish between an argument used to debate a difference of opinion and an argument used to ventilate anger and hostility. Whites misinterpret Black intentions to solve a disagreement and do not believe Blacks who want to solve a disagreement. "Blacks communicate in debates by becoming high-keyed, animated, interpersonal, and confrontational, while middle-class [W]hites communicate in debates by becoming low-keyed, dispassionate, impersonal, and non-challenging" (Kochman, 1981, p.18).

Classroom disruptions have a direct impact on student attendance and student achievement. In the same study, it was revealed that classroom disruptions increased both student absences and tardiness in addition to decreasing student classroom grades. According to Figure 1, when there is a classroom disruption, the teacher submits a student misconduct referral to the Assistant Principal or designee. The designee evaluates the referral and may assign a consequence. When the consequence is an In-School Suspension, the student makes the choice to be either late for school, or absent from school. The lateness or absence from the school then results in a decrease in classroom grades. The decrease in classroom grades results in increased classroom disruption incidents with the same teacher who submitted the referral.

Classroom disruption consequences cause adolescents to develop oppositional behaviors to school expectations. As a result, Black students are convinced that White teachers are racist and prejudiced, and thus reject White teachers' authority due to their experience with racism. In the next chapter I, will discuss the thinking pattern for the teachers and students who were involved in classroom disruptions.

Figure 1.

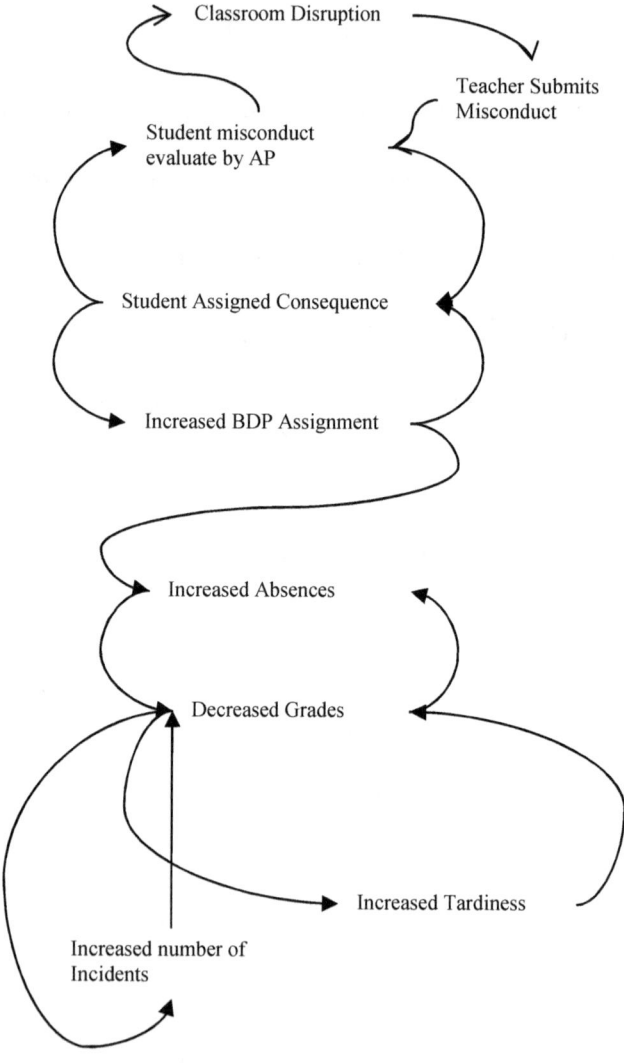

DISRUPTIVE MENTALITY

Successful classroom racism management results in teachers bringing the best out of their students. Bringing the best out of students requires that teachers have an insight of the challenges associated with classroom disruptions. In this section, you will find the thinking patterns (mental models) for teachers and students who were involved in classroom disruptions. Mental models evaluate the values, attitudes, and beliefs people are thinking that cause a structure to exist.

Teachers believed that teacher-student relationships, student attitudes, and student preparation caused classroom disruptions. One teacher believed teacher-student relationships cause classroom disruptions and stated, "I noticed that there are certain people who have a lot of discipline problems. I watch how they interact with the kids, and they don't have that relationship." Teacher-student conflicts result from a difference in desires, and even though this difference maybe reduced, it remains in schools. The classroom conflict between teachers and students results from the different cultural contexts that students and teachers bring to the classroom.

Some classroom disruptions begin with student attitudes. One teacher stated:

> "I have one student in particular who, whenever she has a bad day, she comes in and she will have the worst attitude. She will not want to do any work, and that could lead to a discipline referral because she is refusing to do [the] work."

As children advance in school, they become "less willing to try, for fear of making mistakes and being embarrassed in front of their peers" (Haberman, 1995, p. 76). Teachers should encourage and praise students for doing their best, regardless of their work when compared to other students. Encouragement has a positive impact on teacher-student relationships in the classroom. Encouragement from teachers in a school setting may enhance student self-esteem, thereby increasing teacher effectiveness.

Teachers can facilitate the development of students' self-esteem by taking a personal interest in them by rewarding them for all successes, and by equating effort with ability. Another teacher stated:

> "I have one student . . . he comes [in] one day, he wants to answer all the questions and do all the work, and he is happy. Another day, he does not want to do [anything]. He is very serious; he does not want anybody to talk to him."

Teachers are sometimes surprised when students do not feel that they are acting inappropriately in the classroom. Another teacher stated:

> "You can tell when they [are going to] refuse to participate. Every time I stand in the door, I say 'hi' to all my students. I stand in the door [to] make sure I make contact with every student before they come to my room. Sometimes, they do not want to say 'hi,' so I know from the door that there is something wrong."

Teachers who engage students one-by-one in casual conversation before class begin to lose most of the students' interest after 20 minutes.

Another teacher believed other challenges cause classroom disruptions. This teacher stated, "The student was tired, not physically ready, or mentally ready to participate in the activity… the more I persisted, the more oppositional the student became." While teachers believed that students were the root cause for classroom disruptions, students had a different view.

Many students who exhibit this way of thinking are considered resistive, and teachers who use coercion, an attempt to manage students by applying sanctions such as detention, suspension, and corporal punishment, are ineffective when working with resistant students. Resistant students view this as the boss using coercion and become the teacher's adversaries.

One way to work with a resistant student is to help them identify their feelings associated with anger, and then teach them an anger coping skill. Recently, a five-year-old was sent to my office for his behavior. I asked him if he was angry, and he replied, "yes." I asked him to give me an angry face; then I asked him to give me a happy face. After he mastered his feelings for anger and happiness, I asked him to practice taking deep breaths. Then, I asked him to make an angry face. Next, I asked him to take a deep breath and then asked him to smile. We practiced this pattern of angry face - deep breathing - happy face - for several minutes and I released him back to class. The next day, his teacher told me that the student was completely different and was well behaved. The teacher told me that she followed up the intervention by giving him praise for his new behavior.

Verbal encouragement by teachers increases student participation and desired behavior. Praise is an effective reinforcement that provides encouragement to students and is reinforcement for behavior performance improvement. Praise is an effective reinforcement that helps to build student self-esteem.

Another great coping skill is to teach students to redirect their anger. I had a student who came to my office because he had been acting up the entire day. When he came to my office, he expressed to me that he was angry with the teacher. I sat him down and taught him that if he wanted to show the teacher that he was a good student, he had to sit with his hands folded. Then, I told him that if he felt angry at the teacher, all he had to do was squeeze his hands. We practiced this for several minutes and I helped him to practice this new coping skill in his classroom.

A student's self-esteem suffers when they develop negative perceptions regarding their teachers. In this study, students believed teacher behaviors caused classroom disruptions. One student stated:

> "That [teacher] was out of control… I [had] already turned around and was doing my work; why [do]

you want me to turn around again? That makes no sense to me. That does not make sense at all." Another student reflected on a teacher's behavior stating, "I used to be in [one teacher's class]. [This teacher] used to kick everybody out for no reason. We all was sitting there, [he would say] 'you are not doing your work, get out.'" Another student stated:

"I was mad because [the teacher] just snapped on me... I really did not do anything. I was just asking what the question was, and [the teacher] did not want to repeat it because I guess he said it so many times."

Another student believed that teachers yelling at students caused classroom disruptions. When a teacher yells, uses harsh words, shames, degrades, or embarrasses a student, such behavior influences all students. Good teachers do not yell at students and give them the opportunity to improve their behavior when they misbehave. Students believe good teachers do not yell, though some Black students believe that caring teachers yell and are strict so long as the teacher does not overuse these strategies.

In addition to students blaming teachers, they also admitted to causing classroom disruptions. One student stated:

> "We got in an argument because I did not want to do the work... I did not understand it. Me not noticing that she was helping everybody else, I wanted her to come directly to me before everybody else. She just wanted me to do it on my own. I balled up the paper and I called her crazy, so I got kicked out of class."

Some minority students may have difficulty with some teachers and school selected classroom instructional materials. Instructional materials and instructors that work well for European students do not necessarily work well for culturally diverse students, and to believe that they do is to assume that Black, Latino, American Indian, Asian, Arab, and African immigrants have identical personal, social, cultural, historical, and family traits. Teachers need to realize that constructed classroom collaboration may be more culturally relevant and meaningful to some students. For instance, cooperative learning structures provide a cultural match for Hispanic students while "African American learning seems to be influenced by the social situation in which learning occurs" (Shade, 1997, p. 23). Blacks prefer to work in groups and socially interactive environments, thus, Black students do well when the teacher incorporates a socialization learning model and "will work together to benefit the group" (Gilbert & Gay, 1985, p. 134). Black students work and function better in cooperative, informal, and loosely structured environments where teachers and students work together to achieve a common goal. When teachers and students work together, they can eliminate classroom disruptions.

Eliminating classroom disruptions requires that educators take a different approach to ensure that the associated devastating impact has minimal impact. As an Assistant Principal, I supervised a teacher who had similar challenges in her classroom. I had recommended to the teacher a process for developing classroom rules with student participation.

The teacher came to me and stated, "Mr. Campbell, I am having so many problems with my sixth-period class, and I do not know what to do." I responded by saying, "Have you tried developing rules and consequences with student input?" After further discussion, she said, "I am going to try it," and a week later, she told me, "That process worked so well with my sixth-period class that I am going to use it with all of my classes."

Essentially, the process involves the teacher and the students developing a shared vision in the area of classroom disruptions. According to Senge (1990):

> "Shared vision is vital for the learning organization because it provides the focus and energy for learning. While adaptive learning is possible without vision, generative learning occurs only when people are striving to accomplish something that matters deeply to them (p. 206)."

Working with students to develop a shared vision regarding classroom disruptions will help teachers to develop cultural knowledge regarding their students.

Researchers have reported challenges with limited teacher cultural knowledge regarding minority students. Teachers who are culturally different from their students have a greater challenge creating a trusting classroom environment when cultural diversity and race factors are not put on the table by the school, and students perceive these factors as important to their identity and school success. Similarly, teachers who have limited knowledge regarding a student are more likely to have low interaction rates with that student. Instructors need student cultural background information because instructors and students "affect attitudes, beliefs and values about education, ideas about how classes ought to be conducted, how students and teachers ought to interact, and what type of relationships are appropriate for students and teachers."

When cultural awareness between White teachers and Black students is absent, the impending result is interference with effective instructional processes caused by frustration and alienation between White teachers and Black students. Students who find their culture and learning styles reflected in instruction are more likely to be motivated and less likely to be disruptive. Good teachers adjust their teaching to serve populations that are culturally and linguistically diverse, which includes incorporating culturally responsive pedagogy by adjusting teaching strategies according to individual learning styles. According to Leiding (2006), "teachers who are sensitive to various cultures will learn about students' backgrounds and ensure that they are aware of relevant information about cultural traditions, religious practices, and patterns of interaction that may affect a student's classroom participation" (p. 279). When teachers realize that learning takes place across cultural mediums, they can then adapt teaching to fit student needs.

I recommend the following steps. First, list all causes for classroom disruptions. The classroom disruption list includes:

1) Excessive talking
2) Talking back
3) Cursing
4) Insubordination
5) Screaming during instruction
6) Students telling other students that they are going to fail
7) Refusing to change seats
8) Throwing a paper ball at another student
9) Clowning and making jokes
10) Using inappropriate language
11) Shouting into a classroom from the hallway
12) Playing cards in the classroom laughing
13) Sleeping in class on a regular basis
14) Throwing a pencil at another student
15) Responding to another student in a disrespectful manner
16) Walking into a class/shop area without permission.

Second, divide students into groups of five and ask them to recommend consequences for each infraction; also ask them to recommend rewards for classes that do not become involved in classroom disruptions as this will provide an opportunity for students to manage themselves. Finally, list the infraction and consequences that the students developed in plain sight for the students.

Teachers can facilitate a process for overcoming the cultural differences between teachers and students that continue to contribute to the need for classroom racism management techniques. The cultural differences between teachers and students will contribute to the overall school climate. In the next section, I will discuss the dilemmas associated with school discipline and racism.

CIVIL RIGHTS IMPASSE

Successful classroom racism management eliminates civil rights allegations against schools and teachers. In recent years, many schools have been faced with civil rights complaints associated with school discipline. According to the Department of Education Office of Civil Rights, if a person believes that a public school, as well as a public or private college or university (which includes vocational schools that receive federal funds) has discriminated against someone on the basis of race, color, national origin, sex, or age, can file a civil rights complaint. The persons must file a complaint within 180 days of the alleged discrimination. Even though many institutions have a grievance process, the individual does not have to use the process and can file the civil rights complaints as a first alternative.

When a civil rights compliant is filed, the investigation can include assessing teacher referrals for discipline. For example, the U.S. Office of Civil Rights visited six Winston-Salem/Forsyth County schools to review whether discipline policies, especially for Black male students were excessive. The schools were asked:

- To describe how they handle discipline
- At what point discipline matters are turned over to an assistant principal
- Who entered discipline information into the computer system

In most cases, the discipline process begins with the submission of a discipline referral from a teacher. Schools will need to better prepare in terms of school discipline to avoid the pitfalls associated with civil rights complaints.

The challenges with school discipline continue to polarize our communities, scholars, and educators. According to Mortimer Adler, "true freedom is impossible without a mind made free by discipline." There exist two schools of thought that polarize the school discipline challenge. Max Eden contends that the middle of the road is an approach is best for addressing challenges associated with school discipline as he believes that "history shows time and time again that it's always possible to go too far when trying to solve a social problems. If we believe that the disparities are due to tractable racial bias and sub-optimal classroom management strategies, then a professional development initiative coupled with a more intentional disciplinary culture would do a great deal of good."

On the other end of the spectrum, Hailly Korman states that "there is no such thing as going to far." She surmised that suspension and expulsion rates far exceed school violence, and that "suspending or expelling disruptive students does not lead to increased school safety, better academic outcomes, or improved school climate."

According to the American Psychological Association (APA), a rigid practice of punitive school removals has, in fact, the opposite effect. The APA reviewed 10 years of zero tolerance policies in middle and high schools, and it was found that zero tolerance policies that were intended to reduce school violence and behavioral problems were ineffective. Zero tolerance policies failed to increase the consistency of discipline across student groups and failed to decrease uneven enforcement of punishment across racial lines.

In one corner, an emphasis is placed on staying in the middle of the road while the other emphasizes extremism.

The suggested strategies for transformation are either outdated or lack depth. Public policy makers attempted to intervene to assist with eliminating civil rights complaints associated with school discipline.

The Obama administration, along with New York City Mayor, de Blasio instituted additional measures to help schools with the school discipline challenges. Mayor de Blasio elected to require principals to seek written permission to suspend students. He also introduced a $1.2 million initiative for training educational staff from 100 NYC schools in restorative justice and the School Climate Leadership Team. The New York City efforts to improve alleged racist school discipline by using restorative justice techniques appears to have failed miserably.

Restorative justice is an approach to justice that focuses on the needs of the victims and the offenders as well as the involved community, instead of satisfying abstract legal principles or punishing the offender. Victims take an active role in the process, while offenders are encouraged to take responsibility for their actions "to repair the harm they've done — by apologizing, returning stolen money, or community service." In addition, it provides help for the offender in order to avoid future offences and is based on a theory of justice that considers crime and wrongdoing to be an offence against an individual or community, rather than the state. The designers believe that restorative justice fosters dialogue between victim and offender and shows the highest rates of victim satisfaction and offender accountability.

The problem with their plan to eliminate school discipline is that it does not empower the frontline persons such as the teachers. The decision is paramount to a power over decision for which many politicians and educators make their decisions. They made this decision because their basic belief is that the educators are too lazy or unwilling to improve school discipline. Therefore, they emphasize tight controls, threats, and punishments.

One example of this leadership usage was the threat to public schools through a "Dear Colleague" letter. In January 2014, the U.S. Department of Education issued a "Dear Colleague" letter that advised school districts that if their school discipline policy "is neutral on its face — meaning that the policy itself does not mention race — and is administered in an evenhanded manner but has a disparate impact, i.e., a disproportionate and unjustified effect on students of a particular race, they could become the subject of a federal civil rights investigation for unlawful discrimination."

In response to the letter regarding school discipline, twenty-seven states revised their laws which caused school suspension rates to plummet. In New York City, there were 53,504 suspensions during the 2013–14 school year, however, during the 2015–16 school year, that number had fallen to 37,647, a decline of more than 29 percent.

However, this decrease in school discipline was not without casualties. For example, minority high school students were impacted by the new school discipline regulations. Since 2013, the reading scores for minority students have plummeted from a passing rate of 71.2%, to a rate of 60.2%. Furthermore, since 2013, the math scores for minority students have also plummeted from a passing rate of 67.4%, to a rate of 49.9%.

Another casualty to the new school discipline efforts were the teachers. The new school discipline training policy widened the gap between the students' perceptions and the teachers intentions. For example, during cultural sensitivity training, a requirement of school districts under restorative justice programs, teachers were told they are largely to blame for bad behavior of Black students because they "misinterpret" African-American culture. In addition, the following course description infuses a continued widening of this gap. "Institutions are infested with token people of color and racist white people who uphold White Supremacy, causing a survivor mentality among those who encounter daily micro-invalidations, -aggressions, and -assaults in hostile environments. Through a historical overview, learn about the oppressive system known as the American Education System, a school system that was never designed for children of color."

As a teacher, your first response is to become defensive. However, when teachers become defensive they will reject the efforts that are causing the defensiveness. In this instance, teachers continued to blame the students, the parents, the administrators, and the community.

This is known to be true because of several responses to the new discipline policies in other regions in the country. For example, a Los Angeles Unified School District is seeing a similar spike in campus offenses after its school superintendent followed federal orders to reduce suspensions of African-Americans - even threats against teachers are ignored, as administrators' hands are tied by the new policy.

Another teacher exclaimed that "I was terrified and bullied by a fourth-grade student," a teacher at a Los Angeles Unified School District (LAUSD) school recently noted on the Los Angeles Times website. "The black student told me to 'Back off, b—h.' I told him to go to the office and he said, 'No, b—h, and no one can make me... I'm going to torture you. I'm doing this because I can't be removed.'"

Complaints from another LAUSD teacher was, "We now have a 'restorative justice' counselor, but we still have the same problems. Kids aren't even suspended for fights or drugs." In neighboring Orange County, teachers are dealing with increasingly violent and disrespectful student behavior since schools there have also switched to the restorative strategy.

The school discipline challenge is a product of a dysfunctional relationship between teachers and students. The primary focal point of teaching is simple – it is the relationship between a teacher and a group of kids, so any educational reform initiatives such as improving school discipline is bound to fail if the importance of teacher-student classroom relationships is neglected. Dysfunctional relationships begin with the values that we develop to ensure that we do not suffer from circumstances that upset, embarrass, or threaten individuals.

From a historical perspective, Blacks feel threatened due to cultural racism. Cultural racism results from the dominant, or more powerful group defining cultural values and value characteristics. Anti-Black prejudice in America has historical roots in slavery, carpetbagging, and the failure of Reconstruction in the South after the Civil War. The army set the stage for labeling Blacks as inferior by using the Alpha and Beta test that contained a number of visual information processing tasks that Blacks were not proficient at.

This has led some minorities to believe they cannot trust White institutions, and, as a result, adolescents may develop oppositional social identities that are contrary to the social expectations of mainstream society when they experience racism and respond with anger and rebellion. Black students have become convinced that White teachers are racist and prejudiced, and therefore reject White teachers' authority due to their experience with racism.

Since teachers are hired to educate all children, this projected attitude can threaten the quality of life for many teachers, and many teachers respond by altering their expectations of Black students. Teachers are more likely to have negative academic and behavioral expectations regarding Black students when compared to expectations of White students. White teachers have more negative attitudes toward Black children and rate Black students more negatively when compared to White students.

This "protection" of quality of life also impacts European American teachers causing European American teachers to favor other students rather than Black students. European Americans have favorable attitudes toward Mexican Americans when compared to Blacks and are more likely to accept Mexican Americans when compared to Blacks due to Mexican Americans having a closer skin color to European Americans.

Overcoming the challenges associated with school discipline will require schools to take an alternative approach. There is only one transitional model that will improve relationships between teachers and students. Schools should use both the "Raccelerate Formula," and the "Promoting Positive Racial Teacher Student Classroom Relationships" transitional model created by Dr. Campbell. In the next section, I will discuss the Raccelerate Formula.

THE RACCELERATE FORMULA

The Raccelerate Formula is a classroom racism management tool that helps educators to avoid the atrocities associated with allegations of racism that result from school discipline. The Classroom Racism Exterminator unveiled the Raccelerate Formula and the Raccelerate Scale on February 24, 2015. The Raccelerate Racism Formula helps teachers and schools to determine where they fall on the Raccelerate Racism Scale. The Raccelerate Racism Formula and the Raccelerate Racism Scale are direct products of the Raccelerate Phenomenon.

The Raccelerate Phenomenon has roots in Newton's Third Law of Motion. Newton's Third Law of Motion states that when one body exerts a force on a second body, the second body simultaneously exerts a force equal in magnitude and opposite in direction on the first body. In elementary terms, Newton's Third Law of Motion states that for every action there is an equal and opposite reaction.

The Raccelerate Phenomenon follows the same principle as Newton's Third Law of Motion in that whenever there is a perceived infringement by a Black male against a White female there is an negative overreaction portrayed in the media. Specifically, the Raccelerate Phenomenon states that for every action that a Black male takes against a White female there is an elevated negative reaction towards the Black male. The Raccelerate Phenomenon is the cause for many of the racial tensions between Blacks and Whites.

Recently, there were a number California school districts that were identified as racist because they were over disciplining Black students. It appears that California schools that had more than 200 recorded incidents were classified as racist and were provided the additional training. Using this as a threshold, thirty-two schools qualified for the additional diversity training.

The problem with using this type of evaluation is that some schools that were in need of additional training, according to their standards, were not provided the services because they did not meet the required 200 minimum disciplinary infractions. For example, Wheatland Union High School had 144 suspensions for 738 students. For this school the suspension rate was 15.45%. This is well above the national average of 7%. Another school that would have benefited from the additional training is Colfax Elementary. This school had 41 suspensions for 582 students. For this school the suspension rate was 7.04%. Additionally, there were 27% of the schools that were above the national average.

A better way to evaluate the California schools would have been to utilize the Normal Distribution Curve. In probability theory, the normal (or Gaussian) distribution is a very common continuous probability distribution. Normal distributions are important in statistics and are often used in the natural and social sciences to represent real-valued random variables whose distributions are not known.

The normal distribution is useful because of the central limit theorem. In its most general form, under some conditions (which include finite variance), it states that averages of random variables independently drawn from independent distributions converge in distribution to the normal, that is, become normally distributed when the number of random variables is sufficiently large. Physical quantities that are expected to be the sum of many independent processes (such as measurement errors) often have distributions that are nearly normal. Moreover, many results and methods (such as propagation of uncertainty and least squares parameter fitting) can be derived analytically in explicit form when the relevant variables are normally distributed.

The normal distribution is represented by the bell curve. The bell curve refers to the shape that is created when a line is plotted using the data points for an item that meets the criteria of normal distribution. The center contains the greatest number of a value and therefore would be the highest point on the arc of the line. This point is referred to the mean.

The important things to note about a normal distribution is the curve is concentrated in the center and decreases on either side. The bell curve signifies that the data is symmetrical and thus we can create reasonable expectations as to the possibility that an outcome will lie within a range to the left or right of the center, once we can measure the amount of deviation contained in the data .

The following figure reveals the normal distribution curve for the information provided in the article - California's school suspensions show racial disparity (USA Today, February, 2015).

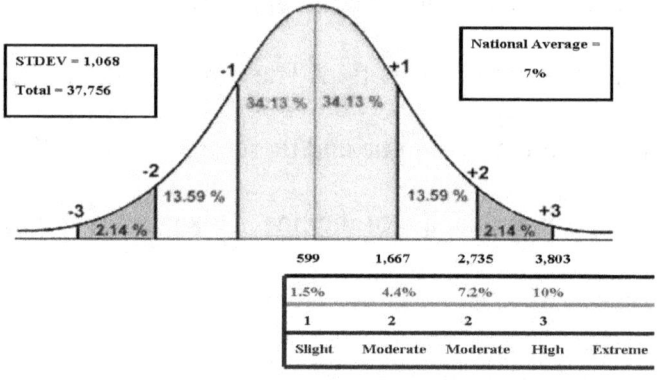

The normal distribution curve reveals that the average rate for suspensions was 1.5%. This equates to 50% of the schools had a suspension rate of 1.5%. At the +1 standard deviation the suspension rate was 4.4%. This equates to

34.13% of the schools had a suspension rate from 1.5% to 4.4%. At the +2 standard deviation the suspension rate was 7.2%. This equates to 13.59% of the schools had a suspension rate from 4.4% to 7.2%%. At the +3 standard deviation the suspension rate was 10%. This equates to 2.14% of the schools had a suspension rate from 7.2% to 10% which also exceeded the national out of school suspension rate.

These schools would have benefited from using the Raccelerate Formula. The Raccelerate Formula is designed to prevent the perception of racism. For the California schools that were at 1.5% they would have received a slight rating. This means that the perception of racism in schools is slight. For those schools that were between 4.4% and 7.2% they would have received a 2 rating which is equivalent to moderate. This moderate rating means that the school or teacher is now on the fence of being perceived as racist. For the schools that were above 7.2%, the perception of racism goes from high to extreme. The Raccelerate Formula will help educators to reflect on their practice before any allegations of racism are formally made.

The Raccelerate Racism Formula provides schools a formula for determining possible racism against students in their school or school district. The symbol for the Raccelerate Racism Formula is denoted: RRF

School Version

RRF = Ln ((Number of Students Suspended)/ Total Number of Students) + 5.4

Ln = Natural Log

The Raccelerate Racism Scale is a 0 to 10 numerical scale.

RRF	
0-1	Not Racist
1-2	Slightly Racist
2-3	Moderately Racist
3-4	Highly Racist
4-10	Extremely Racist

Teacher Version

RRF = Ln ((Number of Student Discipline Referrals)/ Total Number of Students) + 5.4

Ln = Natural Log

The Raccelerate Racism Scale is a 0 to 10 numerical scale.

RRF	
0-1	Not Racist
1-2	Slightly Racist
2-3	Moderately Racist
3-4	Highly Racist
4-10	Extremely Racist

The Raccelerate Formula provides schools and teachers an opportunity to reflect on the discipline priorities in their classroom and school before any allegations of racism surface. Unlike many other programs, it provides the school or teacher with the power to eliminate any discipline problems that will associate them with allegations of racism. Another factor that can contribute to allegations of racism is the communication process between teachers and students. In the next chapter, I will discuss effective classroom communication.

EFFECTIVE CLASSROOM COMMUNICATION

Effective classroom racism management involves effective communication. Education is a communication process that is not limited to transmitting knowledge but also involves interpersonal communication behaviors and nonverbal behaviors that are the major aspects of interpersonal relationships, which are critical in all learning situations. The teaching-learning process is essentially a communication event that includes verbal and nonverbal communication. Teachers and students are verbal and nonverbal message senders and receivers. Effective classroom racism management with students requires considerable knowledge of their verbal and nonverbal communication styles.

Schools and Black student conflict develop from expectation differences related to communication styles. The general public fails to accept that Blacks have different communication norms and conventions by assuming that Blacks communicate using standards set by socially dominant Whites. Whites' dispassionate and detached communication mode creates distrust among Blacks due to its similarity to Blacks who front which occurs when Blacks perceive there is a communication risk factor and chooses to remain silent in Black-White communication encounters. Most Black educational failure arises from the teachers' inability to understand how the students communicate. According to Brown (2003), "Urban educators must be aware of specific verbal and nonverbal communication styles that affect students' ability and motivation to engage in learning activities (p. 280).

The consideration of student verbal behaviors for the success of classroom racism management. Black verbal communication styles can influence teacher-student classroom relationships. White Americans' unfamiliarity with the Black communication style results in a misunderstanding by the American mainstream. According to Gay and Abrahams (1972):

> The majority of culture in the schools arises because of differences in the communication and interaction system. Lower-class Blacks in the United States do not communicate the same way other Americans do and that troubles us a good deal. It especially irritates those of us who have operated most of our lives on the assimilationist ideal – the melting pot set of expectations – and must include a great majority of teachers in this country. (p. 69)

Blacks not only debate the idea; they also debate the person while Whites debate the idea rather than the person debating the idea. "Blacks often probe beyond a given statement to find out where a person is "coming from," in order to clarify the meaning and value of a particular behavior or attitude" (Kochman, 1981, p. 23). Black students contrast White middle-class communication when they speak over others' voices and repeat the communication until they are responded to or until they have someone's attention. Patton et al. (1993) reported:

> Spontaneity in conversation is an acceptable component of [Black] communication, although others perceive interrupting another speaker in conversation as rude. Speaker and audience are often interchangeable as a [Black] listener will often "call out" or respond to a speaker. (p. 10)

Black communities accept the approach that their children use by interrupting others or speaking out of turn, which is an unacceptable school practice, and teachers view this behavior as disruptive and inappropriate (Hanna, 1988). Anglo Americans place a high value on allowing one person at a time to speak to indicate respect for an individual (Milburn, 2000).

Black children's socialization process includes achieving direction through indirection by saying one thing and doing another, which includes using metaphors and symbolism to approach issues in a roundabout manner. Blacks will tell European Americans what they want to hear, which may not be the truth, when pressured. Blacks verbally communicate by using a preponderance of words that denote action and unrestricted movement and by telling the truth or telling it like it is. Black communities view truth-telling or telling it-like-it-is verbal communication as courageous and honest, and a refusal to compromise integrity. Anglo European cultures view this communication as confrontational. Teachers find that attempts to communicate with difficult students may become strained, difficult, or awkward, and therefore such attempts can become impossible.

Black students use several verbal techniques to discover a teacher's strengths and weaknesses in order to evaluate a teacher's racial attitudes and locate teachers' breaking points to help the students empower themselves in the situation between them and the teacher. Abrahams and Gay (1972) reported:

> If a [Black student] expects to rise to the position of a leader, he must know how to keep his cool. If he cannot respond to a [teachers challenge] without becoming frustrated and unnerved, he is not likely

to have the respect of others or remain a leader for long. (p. 205)

"When Blacks are working hard to keep it cool, it signals that the chasm between is getting wider, not smaller" (McCarty, 1981, p. 20). According to Gay (2000):

> Black Students "gain the floor" or get participatory entry into conversations through personal assertiveness, the strength of the impulse to be involved, and persuasive power of the point they wish to make, rather than waiting for "authority" to grant permission. (p. 91)

In the classroom, Black students power play by loud talking or back-talking to make teachers lose their cool and get the last word in. Black students believe teachers show them respect by addressing them as Mr., Mrs., Sir, or Ma'am. Ignoring cultural differences between Blacks and Whites exists when attempting to understand Black and White communication failures. Some Black students engage in verbal communicative activities that may inhibit positive teacher-student classroom relationships development as well as Hispanic students.

Hispanic students use specific language and speech patterns that may contribute to classroom disruptions. Puerto Ricans involved in the decision-making process may use rising intonation, qualifiers, questions, and hedges. Puerto Ricans make decisions jointly where one person speaks and others join in and respond until the group makes a decision. Anglo Americans value one person speaking at a time to indicate respect for the individual. Puerto Ricans use indirectas, a form of speech, which is an indirect way of making something known. Morris (1981) reported:

Indirectas are literally, indirect statements critical of others – insinuations, innuendo. They are disguised or purposely vague to any but the initiated, but clear in meaning to the ones who know the circumstance or the people involved. In form they do not give away either the person speaking or the person spoken of; they seem not to be barbed and directed to particulars, but they are meaningful in context. Anyone who is "in the know" does know how they are applied. (p. 102)

Hispanic students are more likely to participate in group consensus decisions rather than democratic processes. According to Patton et al. (1993):

Lively exchanges with interjections from all those involved are often found in Hispanic-American conversations, individuals do not need to wait for a pause to enter the discussion. Interruptions are

>interpreted as eagerness, involvement, and interest regarding the topic. (p. 11)

Educators "assume that a child who is still and quiet has a better chance of learning than one who is noisy and active" (Parker & French, 1971, p. 277). White teachers may have difficulties in understanding minority students due to differences in dialect and language. Instructors can adapt to cultural differences by recognizing specific speaking pattern preferences and norms.

Classroom racism management techniques include teacher verbal communication. Excellent communication skills ranks as one of the top three most important skills needed by teachers. Teachers have an opportunity to convey to students that the teachers care about such students by:

a. Talking to students at the end of the week regarding some shared topic or at the end of a unit

b. Talking to students when they are working on assignments

c. Commenting in a positive and affirming manner

d. Talking to students at the beginning and end of the school week

Teachers can enhance students' feelings by talking to them. Some Black students believe that caring teachers yell and are strict, as long as the teacher does not overly use these strategies. Most American classrooms involve teacher-student exchanges in which teachers are clear, direct, explicit, and linear with their instruction and students are clear, direct, and explicit with their responses to questions. Successful Hispanic students expect teachers to deliver information clearly, avoid showing any racial or ethnic discrimination, and care about their students. Effective teachers vary voice, movement, and pace to refocus wandering student attention. Teachers often respond to Hispanic students in louder and higher-pitched voices. Effective teachers minimize blameworthy behaviors by criticizing students less while ineffective teachers criticize students more.

Teachers are more likely to criticize poor work and poor answers. Teachers who constantly correct students during reading assignments inhibit them from absorbing the meaning of the readings. Better teachers do not have nervous mannerisms in their speech when under pressure, and when under pressure, they remain relaxed so that the rhythm of their speech is unaffected. Teachers who perceive students as high achievers tend to use more words and speak in a tone that is more positive to these students.

Teachers who engage students one on one in casual conversation before class begins lose most of the students' interest after 20 minutes.

Teachers use praise to engage students in the learning process. Verbal encouragement by teachers increases student participation and desired behavior. Praise is an effective reinforcement that provides encouragement to students and is reinforcement for behavior performance improvement. Praise is an effective reinforcement that helps to build student self-esteem.

Teachers are more likely to praise good answers and good work rather than poor answers or poor work. Teachers praise Hispanic students less and give them less feedback for answering questions correctly as well as appropriate performances. Mexican American mothers with higher education and income levels use praise and inquiry to teach their children while less educated Mexican American mothers with lower incomes use more modeling to teach their children. Black gifted achievers receive less attention, are least praised, and most criticized in a classroom, even when compared to their nonachieving and nongifted Black counterparts. Black students receive less attention, and praise, and receive more criticism when compared to nongifted Blacks while the same teachers treat gifted Whites more positively than nongifted Whites. Black children react more favorably to praise while White children react more to reproof.

Teachers give more praise and less criticism to opposite race children. In classes where the teacher and students are not of the same race, praise is significantly increased while classes where the teacher and student have the same race, praise is significantly decreased. However, White teachers were judged more pleased with praising White students rather than praising Black students, and White females enrolled in a child development course for perspective elementary school teachers who taught a lesson for a group of fourth-, seventh-, and eighth-grade students praised Black students less. Some students believe praise is a punishment. Teachers should encourage and praise students for doing their best, regardless of their work when compared to other students.

Praise can reduce motivation if used when students are performing the desired behavior. Teachers praise students more when students are having trouble mastering the material even though they are working hard or when the students display unacceptable disruptive behavior rather than praise students who are quiet, comforting, well-adjusted, and high achieving. Teachers perceive students whom the teachers wish to remove from their classrooms as low achievers, and these students alienate teachers by continual defiance and disobedience, which causes teachers to respond with frequent praise to make up for negative behavior. However, students whom teachers believe are a joy to teach receive more praise and less criticism in the classroom when compared to other students. Students are able to get teachers to praise them by bringing completed assignments to teachers and exhibiting qualities such as confidence, sociability, and extroversion. Students reward teachers for their praise by smiling and beaming positively. Philosophical objections to praise result from teachers who desire to develop egalitarian relationships with their students and teachers who want to develop independent thinking in their students so that students are less dependent on the teacher. Praise is an effective reinforcement that provides encouragement to students, helps to build student self-esteem, and helps to build close teacher-student classroom relationships.

Humor is a positive way to enhance classroom racism management. Humor can build and strengthen teacher-student classroom relationships, especially on the individual level. Humor is used to:

a. Connect the speaker with the audience, such as the teacher and the student clarify a view or idea
b. Level criticisms so the speaker can continue to identify with the audience to include reinforcing class rules and expectations for normative behaviors
c. Contrast the views of others with themselves, which teachers use as sarcasm or teasing

Humor increases the connection between the teacher and the student when it reduces tensions between the teacher and the student and reveals that the teacher is also human.

Humor results from teachers, who attempt to connect to students personally, stimulate the learning experience, use humor as an alternative to authoritarian discipline, and encourage risk-taking and higher-level thinking. Humor is effective for students who are not interested or motivated in the instructional topic. Humor can motivate students who are bored, stressed, or have negative attitudes toward school and add meaning to the instructional topic. Teachers believe:

    a. Humor shows students teachers are human and can make mistakes

    b. Humor should never embarrass, ridicule, or harm the student

c. Purposeless humor can result in student misbehavior and waste valuable instructional time

Humor helps students learn when used effectively and appropriately. In classrooms where teachers encourage laughter, students learn and retain more information. Humor is ineffective when students are already motivated. Teachers must use humor naturally, or else it can backfire. Teachers who use irrelevant jokes and humor reduce instructional time. Teachers can damage students' self-esteem by joking about a student's name. Mexican Americans use jokes and humor to avoid disagreements. Blacks and Mexican Americans verbally communicate by using jokes and humor.

Teachers are more likely to use humor with mature students. Teachers usually incorporate some type of humor in their instruction with students who will respond enthusiastically. Teachers develop similarity and identification with students when students respond positively to jokes and stories. Teachers lower their personal status and raise student status by making fun of themselves. Middle-school teachers can use humor to build rapport, empower learners, promote problem solving, create interest, enhance student self-esteem, and emphasize socialization. Most interviewed high school students removed from class for behavioral challenges indicate positive teacher characteristics include a sense of humor. Humor results from the realization that a mistake was made that is not bad or harmful.

However, sarcasm will damage classroom racism management. Children believe sarcastic messages are negative. One form of sarcasms is racist remarks.

Teachers believe sarcasm may psychologically damage children. According to Bryant and Zillman (1988), sarcasm and ridicule "may serve a corrective function, the long-term consequence of diminished esteem in the eyes of students may make the immediate gains in terms of behavioral correction not worth the costs" (p. 72). Interviews with high school students removed for behavioral challenges indicate antagonistic and humiliating teacher behaviors include sarcastic responses. Teachers believe students have greater understanding of vocal contradictions and sarcasm as grade level increases. Older children are better at decoding discrepant nonverbal cues when they are attached to sarcastic messages. Criticism decreases student performance.

Teacher sarcasm can devastate the classroom racism management process. Teachers need to develop strategies that will develop effective classroom racism management. Teachers can reveal something regarding themselves to begin this process.

Effective teacher-student interactions involve teachers revealing something regarding themselves that students do not know about their teachers. This influences the relationship between the teacher and the student, and eventually influences how the students feel regarding the content. Students respond to teachers who are personable and social, and make learning fun and relevant. Self-disclosure is likely to have a positive impact when used by teachers to illustrate a concept, reveal a struggle, or show difficulty learning a concept. Good teachers are more likely to engage in disclosure statements that reflect concern for students while poor teachers disclosure statements are evaluative or reflect a negative outlook.

Interviewed teachers, students, and administrators believe teachers who implement effective classroom racism management with students have the ability to make enough self-disclosures that students perceive their teachers as genuine, place an emphasis on mutual respect, and find the right balance between being firm, friendly, and fair. Blacks build trust slowly with European Americans, especially after encountering negative stereotyping and discrimination. When dominant culture persons deny or diminish information regarding Blacks or misrepresent their experiences, then Blacks will not self-disclose. European Americans are disappointed when Blacks do not trust them and disclose information early in a relationship.

According to Powell and Caseau (2004), "students from Euro-American backgrounds probably disclose the most in class. Students from high-context cultures are less likely to engage in self-disclosure. Native Americans, Asians, and

Latinos are less likely to engage in self-disclosure or feel that it is appropriate" (p. 123). Blacks stop self-disclosing and hesitate to self-disclose when others are partially committed to listening and understanding. When European Americans consistently demonstrate trustworthiness, then Blacks will truthfully self-disclose. Self-disclosure may require that teachers and students engage in a question and answer communication process.

Teacher questioning techniques can influence teacher-student classroom relationships. When teachers ask respectful questions, students feel they are in a trusting environment that makes them sense that they are safe. Questions that humiliate students diminish student confidence. Teachers who ask trick questions respond in an arrogant or derogatory manner when students do not respond. Teachers who ask questions to boost their egos will not gain students' respect or admiration. Stupid questions are insulting and can cause anger and frustration. Black students do not appreciate when teachers ask direct personal questions.

Black and Hispanic students have cultural experiences that can impede classroom question-and-answer sessions. Cultural conflicts between the teacher and Black students may surface because of basic question-and-answer sessions because question-and-answer sessions develop when an adult is angry with them. Blacks learn that question-and-answer sessions result when an adult is angry with them, and this process may inhibit students from classroom involvement. Mexican American students respond only when spoken to, initiate only to ask academic questions, and fail to volunteer responses or make other types of questions or comments in the regular classroom. Mexican American students are more likely to direct comments and questions to teachers for guidance and receive fewer product questions and affirmation following correct answers when compared to Anglo American students. Mexican American children's achievement is positively correlated to teacher affirmation after a correct answer.

Educators who react negatively to student call response behaviors may strain classroom racism management efforts. The Black verbal response pattern is usually unnoticed by Whites. Black students may request a speaker, such as a teacher, to repeat the information several times because of disbelief or surprise or as a compliment to the speaker. Denying a Black student's request for assistance and request to repeat information that results from the student's inability to handle Standard English may cause complete withdrawal from the educational process. Blacks receive less verbal contact indicating that their responses are correct, acceptable, or appropriate from White teachers when compared to White students. Hispanics are often ignored or given less time to respond to teachers' questions. Teachers often ignore Hispanic children, and if teachers call on Hispanic children, the teachers implement less wait time for responses when compared with other children and call on them using louder and higher-pitched voices, which indicate that the teachers are irritated. Students increase involvement in classroom discussions when teachers respond to wrong answers by working with the student instead of rejecting the answer outright. Black and Hispanic student verbal classroom behaviors can classroom racism management.

Cultural differences can affect classroom racism management when debates occur in the classroom. Blacks and Whites ignore communication failures because Blacks and Whites assume they are communicating with the standards set by socially dominant Whites. For Whites, the purpose of an argument is to ventilate anger and hostility.

"Blacks distinguish between an argument used to debate a difference of opinion and an argument used to ventilate anger and hostility" (Kochman, 1981, p.18). Whites misinterpret Black intentions to solve a disagreement and do not believe Blacks who want to solve a disagreement. "A request from a Black person to a white person may be encountered as a demand". Blacks communicate in debates by becoming high-keyed, animated, interpersonal, and confrontational while middle-class Whites communicate in debates by becoming low-keyed, dispassionate, impersonal, and non-challenging. The difference in Black and Hispanic, and White debating behavior can cause classroom arguments between minority students and White teachers which can make classroom racism management difficult for teachers.

Some in-class arguments between teachers and Black students are a product of the Blacks system of language socialization that involves students talking, which gets others in the group to listen and respond. One of the most common student classroom infractions is talking. Black students are inclined to talk back when motivated by what a teacher says. Black students may become so impressed with the speaker, such as a teacher, that students will want to hear the speaker again due to an interest in how it was said. Black students also exhibit affective classroom behavior that can influence classroom racism management.

Many Black students want to create the appropriate mood and setting before beginning to work on a task by asking the teacher to repeat the directions. Blacks will argue for recognition of unsuccessful efforts toward completing a task. Many teachers do not expect Black students to interrupt the class by talking to their neighbors and speak without raising their hands. Educators assume quiet students are successful and receive rewards for making teaching an easier task. Teachers respond to students talking in the classroom without permission by ordering, reprimanding, involving students in work, and naming the student. When a teacher yells, uses harsh words, shames, degrades, or embarrasses a student, such behavior influences all students. Teachers who use coercion, an attempt to manage students by applying sanctions such as detention, suspension, and corporal punishment, are ineffective when working with resistant students. Resistant students view this as the boss using coercion and become the teacher's adversaries.

Most teachers react to students as authoritarians when involved in conflict situations. Teachers who use excessive authority may psychologically damage children. When working with difficult students, most teachers focus their conversations on what the students are lacking by coercing, reminding, or lecturing the students on what they should be doing, which does not help with classroom racism mangement and can make matters worse.

Demanding that students submit to teacher authority may result in increased student disruption, therefore decreasing time spent in the learning process. Hispanic students may feel insulted, angry, or resentful, and lose a desire to cooperate or conform as well as lose respect for the educator. Students whom teachers want removed from class are more likely to receive criticism from the teacher when seeking individual assistance and for classroom behavior and work. Teachers can better implement classroom racism management techniques by positive responses to culturally different verbal behaviors.

Classroom racism management requires considering the role that teacher-student non-verbal behaviors influence classroom management. Nonverbal classroom communication is more important than verbal classroom behavior. Nonverbal communication contributes significantly to communicative interpersonal interactions when compared to verbal communication. Nonverbal communication has greater significance than verbal communication that results from nonverbal communication, having a greater impact:

  a. In determining interpersonal context meaning
  b. When accurately determining feelings and emotions
  c. When revealing meanings and intentions that are deception and distortion free
  d. When attaining high-quality communications that represent a much more effective communication medium

e. Represent a more suitable means of communication when compared to verbal communication

According to Richmond (2002):

> The primary function of teachers' nonverbal behavior in the classroom is to improve affect or liking for the subject matter, teacher, and class and to increase the desire to learn more about the subject matter. ... When the teacher improves affect through effective nonverbal behavior, then the students are more likely to listen more, learn more, and have a more positive attitude about the school. (p. 70)

Students who perceive that teachers feel favorable toward them demonstrate desired classroom behaviors. Students are more likely to complete assignments in classes that they feel accepted by the teacher.

Nonverbal communication includes three interacting systems, the visual, auditory, and invisible communication systems. Auditory communication involves loudness, pitch, rate, duration, quality, regularity, articulation, pronunciation, and pitch. Visual communication is the most important nonverbal communication system, and includes kinesthetic, proxemic, and artifactual subsystems. Kinesthetic communication includes facial expression, eye behaviors, gestures, and posture. Proxemic communication involves the use of space, distance, and territory for communication purposes. Artifactual communication involves facial and bodily appearances and the options that communicators use to alter their appearance. Individuals who nonverbally communicate in a manner consistent with a culture are perceived as more interpersonally attractive by members of that culture. Teachers who identify, analyze, and modify, if necessary, their nonverbal behavior improve their effectiveness. Teachers can learn to become effective by attending and completing a teacher preparation programs offered at colleges.

Colleges teach teachers to ensure there is a distance between themselves and the students so the teacher can maintain discipline in the classroom. European Americans are more likely to have close social distance with Mexican Americans when compared to Blacks and prefer to keep their personal space at arm's length. Hispanic Americans stand close to or side by side instead of face-to-face when talking to another person. Hispanic Americans stand 6 to 8 inches within an arm's length when talking to another person. Latinos interact at a close distance and frequently touch one another. Latino Americans prefer closer standing distances when compared to North Americans. Blacks prefer closer social distance when compared to Mexican Americans. Blacks are more likely to touch each other in a conversation when compared to Whites. Individuals who perceive a proximity violator as someone who will provide them with negative rewards will react negatively when the proximity violator moves closer. Maintaining the appropriate or comfortable proximity is associated with a positive effect, friendship, and attraction.

Teachers who are sensitive to various cultures will learn about student interaction patterns that may affect student classroom participation. A United States North Carolina primary school teacher used a unique handshake ritual to have positive interactions with his students. The Ashley Park Elementary School English teacher interacted with students using a handshake based on the different personalities of each student. The interaction routine was conducted before each class that ranged from understated handshakes, fist pumps, elaborate dance moves, shuffles, and salutes.

Preventing misbehavior and maintaining a positive classroom climate require three to five positive interactions with students to every one negative interaction. Interaction distances increase as children grow older. Interaction space decreases as liking or acquaintance between individuals in a dyad increases. Adolescents interact at closer distances than adults but farther distances than children.

Schools and Black students' conflict develops from expectation differences related to interaction styles. Black children in grades one to four tend to stand closer for communication purposes when compared to other ethnic groups. White Americans believe Blacks should interact with them by acknowledging their cultural identity, being socially polite and friendly, and supporting their arguments while Mexican Americans should interact with them by being socially polite, which includes speaking proper English, showing concern for the other individual, and being assertive and friendly. Black Americans believe Whites should interact with them by being polite to the other as an individual, supporting their arguments and making them relevant, and being assertive. Mexican Americans believe Whites should interact with them by being socially polite, showing concern for the individual, acknowledging their cultural identity, being friendly, staying on topic, and showing openness.

Black and White teachers provide Black male students with more interactions such as criticism, question-and-response non-acceptance, and behavior-controlling questions. Students can assess their academic and social capabilities from classroom interactions. The relationship between classroom interactions and achievement depends upon lesson type, student ability, and the emotional climate of the classroom. Teachers and students may decrease their interaction distance when they feel comfortable with each other, which may influence how teachers assign students seating arrangement within the classroom.

Teachers assign seating for disruptive students first and then assign students who do not have disruptive behavior to sit next to the disruptive students. Disruptive students may interpret seat assignments at the front of the classroom as resulting from a special relationship with the teacher. Insecure and anxious teachers represent their authority by establishing a territory around their desk. Even though teachers have the authority to assign students seating patterns they are still required to facilitate a learning environment that is conducive to high student achievement. Teachers are required to present themselves as friends and facilitators of learning rather than purveyors of knowledge.

Teachers who create a warmer classroom climate for students demonstrate high expectations of by smiling. Effective teachers exhibit enthusiasm by facial expressions, which positively influences student attitudes and student perceptions of teachers. Cognitive learning increases when teachers smile at the class. Teachers who smile are perceived as friendly while a frowning teacher is perceived as mean or grumpy. Frowns from teachers who conduct demanding lessons with high-ability students may indicate a belief that students are capable of excellence while the same frown may indicate low expectations and impatience when the teachers conduct a remedial lesson with slow students.

Individuals use nonverbal cues to indicate a disliking for another individual by unpleasant facial expressions. "Negative emotions are more acceptable when indicated by facial expression in the [Black] culture" (Patton et al.,

1993, p. 9). Blacks have a high sensitivity to facial expressions, which provides them with superior facial expression and other emotion evaluation skills when compared to other ethnic groups. Blacks interpret communication meaning by interpreting facial gestures. Black females pay closer attention to male facial expressions rather than physical characteristics when compared to White females. Teachers should consider Black facial expression evaluation techniques when conveying approval or disapproval to students.

Teacher facial expressions can convey approval or disapproval to students. Black students receive less positive facial attention from White teachers when compared to White students. Black and White teachers demonstrate positive facial expressions toward students of their own culture when compared to students from a different culture.

Frequent smiles are one of many positive signals used in junior and senior high school.

Individuals can also use facial expressions such as eye contact to convey liking for another individual. Individuals use nonverbal cues to indicate a liking for another individual by initiating and maintaining eye contact. Whites believe maintaining eye contact in face-to-face communication is most desirable. White American employees and employers believe maintaining eye contact communicates trustworthiness, masculinity, sincerity, and directedness and conclude when Black employees fail to maintain eye contact that the Black employees have something to hide. European Americans view looking away or looking downward as a sign of disinterest, shyness, or disrespect.

Within Black culture, avoiding eye contact is a sign of disrespect. Some Black parents teach their children that looking an adult in the eye is a sign of disrespect while White children learn to do the opposite.

This is why one particular classroom management technique is ineffective with Black students. In elementary school classroom the usage of "eyes on me" is ineffective. The teacher demands that students respond to their command of 'eyes on me" by stating "eyes on you" and then looking at the teacher. For Black students this is not consistent with what they are taught at home and will lead to distrust between the teacher. Repeated refusal to make eye contact with a White teacher will eventually end a disciplinary consequence for the student. A more suitable alternative is for the teacher to clap at the students in a rhythm form. Then the students are to respond in the same rhythm form. This is more natural for Black students because they are more kinesthetic when compared to other ethnicities.

When reprimanding Black children, they tend not to look at the teacher as a sign of respect. Blacks are less likely to maintain eye contact with persons in a position of authority, and Black children increase eye contact as they begin to trust the teacher. Black students who avert their eyes and verbally express themselves may be just as attentive as White students who gaze directly at the speaker. Students may avoid teacher eye contact when they do not want to be called on or do not know the answer and respond by busily taking notes, rearranging books and papers, and fropping their pencils. Black adults gaze at others when talking to indicate interest. Blacks often "give the eye" as a displeasure indication related to negative feelings. Black eye contact behavior can result in increasing eye contact period when interacting with persons.

Extended eye contact can indicate aggressive anxiety in others. Hispanic students in mainstream classrooms address and respond to teachers clearly, concisely, and require that the teacher look at them. Hispanic students in bilingual classrooms may lower their heads, look away, and giggle. Hispanic Americans view prolonged eye contact as disrespectful. Hispanic American children lower their eyes when reprimanded. Latino Americans believe disagreement expressions and eye contact with senior citizens is rude. Eye contact behavior can influence classroom racism management.

Teachers must also consider how other nonverbal behavior can impact classroom racism management. Teacher and student listening behavior can influence classroom racism management.

Teachers can enhance students' feelings by listening to them. Blacks indicate they are listening by nodding their heads. In the United States, a head nod signifies agreement. In White culture, a perpendicular nod during a conversation indicates an agreement, acceptance, or understanding. In the Black culture, a perpendicular nod during a conversation indicates a conversational catalyst, not an agreement, acceptance, or understanding. Blacks indicate they are listening by making short sounds, and verbally respond to indicate that they are listening. Blacks accept interrupting others or speaking-out-of-turn communicative approach as valued and an indication that the individual is listening, comprehending, and has anticipated the point being made (Shade, 1994). "A Black child may be listening intently, yet to a [W]hite person he gives the appearance of distraction, often because of a different habit of directing his gaze" (Gay & Abrahams, 1972, p. 77). When Black children are thinking of a response, they look away when listening.

Teachers may unknowingly provide inconsistent educational goals that affect students by not considering how they relate to students. Relating to students may require teachers to consider other dynamics that involve teacher-student nonverbal behavior. Teachers may need to consider how physical contact can impact classroom racism management.

Researchers report teachers can relate to students by physical contact. Many teachers do not expect Black students to need a great deal of physical contact. "If an individual such as a teacher touches an African American child, it then becomes acceptable for the child to touch the teacher" (Patton et al., 1993, p. 6). Touching school-aged Blacks on the shoulder, back, arms, or hand is usually reserved for close, intimate relationships with adults. Black students receive less positive physical contact from White teachers when compared to White students. Hispanic Americans pat friends or family on the back or arm when talking. Teachers believe touching between students and teachers decreases as the grade level increases.

Touching between teachers and students can influence classroom racism management development between teachers and students. Teachers and student also exhibit physical behavior regarding their posture. Teacher and student posture behaviors and posture behavior interpretation can influence classroom racism management.

Individuals use nonverbal cues to indicate a disliking for another individual by incongruent postures. Blacks' conversing in a relaxed posture is common. However, a relaxed listening stance may indicate that the listener is tuning out the speaker. Turning away during conversation may also indicate respect and interest or a discussion of personal issues. Cognitive learning increases when teachers have a relaxed body position. Better teachers are more relaxed. Deciphering posture influence requires evaluating nonverbal behavior.

Nonverbal behavior also includes teacher-student physical attributes. Physical attributes can influence teacher-student classroom relationships. "In school settings, teachers seem to expect physically attractive children to be more successful, academically and socially" (Leathers, 1997, p. 144). Because of this expectation, a physically attractive child often becomes the teacher's pet. Students in secondary school settings perceive that dress affects intelligence and academic potential. Taller males and females are perceived by children as stronger when compared to their counterparts.

Teacher physical characteristics can influence classroom racism management. Teachers have the authority to arrange the physical layout for their classrooms. Teachers can increase student motivation by decorating the classroom in a way that is appealing to students. Students who lack motivation attain unsatisfactory levels of learning and become classroom management problems. Enhancing student motivation to enhance classroom racism management requires teachers to prepare physically appealing environments.

REFERENCES

Abrahams, R., & Gay, G. (1972). Talking Back in the Classroom. In R. Abrahams (Ed.), *Language and Cultural Diversity in American Education* (pp. 200-207). Englewood Cliffs, NJ: Prentice Hall.

American Psychological Association (2008). *Are Zero Tolerance Policies Effective in the Schools?* American Psychologist

Arenas, J. (2013). The Inspired Worklife. http://serendipitylabs.com/true-freedom-impossible-without-mind-made-free-discipline-%E2%80%95-mortimer-j-adler/

Berry, S. (2017). *Trump Administration Still Enacting Obama School Discipline Guidance Based on Racial Injustice.* Breibart

Bryant, J., & Zillman, D. (1988). Using Humor to Promote Learning in the Classroom. *Journal of Children in Contemporary Society, 20*(1-2), 49-78.

Gay, G. (2000). *Culturally Responsive Teaching: Theory, Research, and Practice.* New York: Teachers College Press 2000.

Gay, G., & Abrahams, R. (1972). Black culture in the classroom. In R. Abrahams & R. Troike (Eds.), *Language and Cultural Diversity in American Education* (pp. 67-84). Englewood Cliffs: Prentice-Hall.

Haberman, M. (1995). *Star teachers of children in poverty.* West Lafayette, IN: Kappa Delta Pi.

Frederick M. Hess, Frederick M. (2016). *The debate on school discipline.* American   Enterprise Institute

Kochman, T. (1981). *Black and White styles in conflict.* Chicago: University Chicago Press.

Leathers, D. (1997). *Successful Nonverbal Communication: Principles and Applications (3rd).* Boston: Allyn and Bacon.

Leiding, D. (2006). *Racial Bias in the Classroom: Can teachers reach all children?* Lanham, MD: Rowman & Littlefield Education.k

Morris, M. (1981). *Saying and meaning in Puerto Rico: Some problems in the ethnography of discourse* (1st). Oxford, New York: Pergamon Press.

New York City Government (2016). *De Blasio Administration Announces New School Climate Initiatives to Make NYC Schools Safer, Fairer and More Transparent.* http://www1.nyc.gov/office-of-the-mayor/news/628-16/de-blasio-administration-new-school-climate-initiatives-make-nyc-schools-safer-fairer

Patton, D., Warring, D., Frank, K., & Hunter, S. (1993). Multicultural Message: Nonverbal Communication in the Classroom. *ED362519.*

Powell, R., & Caseau, D. (2004). *Classroom Communication and Diversity: Enhancing Instructional Practice.* Mahwah, New Jersey: Lawrence Erlbaum Associates.

Richmond, V. (2002). Teacher nonverbal immediacy: Use and outcomes. In J. Chesebro & J. McCroskely (Eds.), *Communication for Teachers* (pp. 65-82). Boston: Allyn & Bacon.

Senge, P. (1990). The Fifth Discipline: The Art and Practice of the Learning Organization. New York: Doubleday.

Skinner, V. (2015). *POLL: Teachers overwhelmingly oppose Obama's race-based school discipline rules.* EAG News

United States Department of Education, (2017). *How to File a Discrimination Complaint with the Office for Civil Rights.*

https://www2.ed.gov/about/offices/list/ocr/docs/howto.html

United States Department of Education, (2017). Winston-Salem/Forsyth County Schools.

https://www.ed.gov/labor-management-collaboration/conference/winston-salemforsyth-county-schools

www.ingramcontent.com/pod-product-compliance
Lightning Source LLC
Chambersburg PA
CBHW070734230426
43665CB00016B/2235